GEOGRAPHY OF THE WORLD

THE RUGGED
ROCKIES

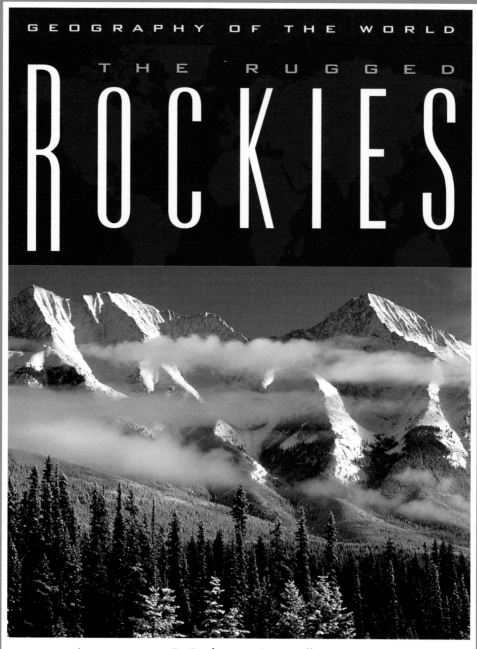

By Barbara A. Somervill

THE CHILD'S WORLD®
CHANHASSEN, MINNESOTA

Published in the United States of America by The Child's World®
PO Box 326, Chanhassen, MN 55317-0326
800-599-READ
www.childsworld.com

Content Adviser:

Mark Williams,

Associate Professor,

University of Colorado,

Boulder, Colorado

Photo Credits: Cover/frontispiece: Gunter Marx Photography/Corbis.
Interior: Animals Animals/Earth Scenes: 15 (Erwin & Peggy Bauer), 21 (Brian K.
Miller), 26 (David Lazenby); Corbis: 4 (David Muench), 6 (Ric Ergenbright), 14
(Gunter Marx Photography), 23 (Lindsay Hebberd), 24 (Lee Cohen), 25 (Lester
Lefkowitz); EyeWire/Punchstock: 10, 17; Photodisc/Punchstock: 18; Picture
Desk/Travelsite: 8 (Colasanti), 11 (Global).

The Child's World®: Mary Berendes, Publishing Director

Editorial Directions, Inc.: E. Russell Primm, Editorial Director; Melissa McDaniel,
Line Editor; Katie Marsico, Associate Editor; Judi Shiffer, Associate Editor and Library
Media Specialist; Matthew Messbarger, Editorial Assistant; Susan Hindman, Copy
Editor; Sarah E. De Capua and Lucia Raatma, Proofreaders; Marsha Bonnoit, Peter
Garnham, Terry Johnson, Olivia Nellums, Chris Simms, Katherine Trickle, and
Stephen Carl Wender, Fact Checkers; Tim Griffin/IndexServ, Indexer; Cian Loughlin
O'Day, Photo Researcher; Linda S. Koutris, Photo Selector; XNR Productions, Inc.,
Cartographer

The Design Lab: Kathleen Petelinsek, Design and Page Production

Library of Congress Cataloging-in-Publication Data
Somervill, Barbara A.
  The rugged Rockies / by Barbara A. Somervill.
    p. cm. — (Geography of the world series)
  Includes index.
  ISBN 1-59296-334-X (library bound : alk. paper) 1. Rocky Mountains—Juvenile
literature. I. Title. II. Series.
  F721.S66 2005
  978—dc22   2004003726

TABLE OF CONTENTS

CHAPTER ONE

PIKE'S MISTAKE

Nearly 200 years ago, President Thomas Jefferson sent Zebulon Pike to explore what is now the American Southwest. On his trip, Pike spotted a mountain that he called the Great Peak. Pike

More people climb Pike's Peak each year than any other mountain in the Rockies.

guessed the peak was 18,000 feet (5,500 meters) high. He and his men tried to climb the mountain, but a snowstorm forced them back to camp. Pike declared that the mountain could not be climbed.

Today, the Great Peak is called Pikes Peak. Pike's ideas about this mountain were very wrong. In 1820, a doctor named Edwin James became the first person known to have climbed Pikes Peak. In 1858, Julia Holmes became the first woman to climb the mountain. By this time, however, the Ute Indians had long been living near Pikes Peak. And in the late 1700s, the Spanish explored the area. Most likely, both the Utes and the Spanish had climbed to the top before either James or Holmes. Today, more people have climbed Pikes Peak than any other mountain in the Rockies.

As for the height, the Great Peak is not so great. Mount Elbert, at 14,433 feet (4,399 m), is the tallest peak in the Rocky Mountains, beating Pikes Peak by 323 feet (98 m). Thirty other Colorado mountains also rise higher than Pikes Peak.

CHAPTER TWO

MAKING A MOUNTAIN RANGE

Mountains are being built all the time. Volcanoes, earthquakes, and intense pressure and massive collisions underground build them up. Wind and water wear them away.

Rock is the basic ingredient in mountains. Rock is made in several ways. Volcanoes produce igneous rock when **magma** cools inside the volcano. **Igneous** rock is very hard. Accumulations of sand,

Powerful forces under the earth's surface twist, buckle, and fold rock such as this.

clay, tiny pieces of rock, or animal remains form **sedimentary** rock. Sedimentary rock is softer than igneous rock. Finally, pressure and heat on existing rocks can form **metamorphic** rock. Metamorphic rock is also fairly hard.

Try this experiment: Take a rock. Pack wet sand around it. Then slowly trickle water over the mound. What happens? The water gradually washes away the sand. Rock is left behind. This is similar to how the Rocky Mountains formed.

Long ago, soft sedimentary rock covered harder rock where the Rocky Mountains are now. Extreme pressure pushed the land higher and higher. As the land rose, it folded, twisted, and buckled. Over millions of years, water and wind wore away the softer, outer layer of sedimentary rock—and left behind mountains of hard rock.

In the Rockies, this process happened several times. The first mountain building happened about 2 billion years ago. Then, 500 million years ago, it happened again. After about 300 million years, an ancient group of Rocky Mountains began to erode into floodplains

CARVING CANYONS

Water erosion is a powerful force. Millions of years ago, a stream began high in the Rocky Mountains. Over time, that stream carved its way through sedimentary rock. That stream became the mighty Colorado River. Its greatest feat was whittling the Grand Canyon. Today, the Grand Canyon stretches for 277 miles (446 kilometers) and is nearly 1 mile (1.6 km) deep. And it all began with a trickle of water!

and sand dunes. Seventy million years ago, a third uplift occurred. This uplift produced today's Rockies.

The Rockies stretch from New Mexico to northeastern British Columbia (Canada). Over this vast distance, many different ecosystems thrive. To the east of the

Melting snow feeds rushing mountain rivers each spring.

Rockies, grasslands rise to about 6,000 feet (1,800 m) above sea level. Short grasses and wildflowers dominate the landscape. Prairie dogs chatter warnings of approaching coyotes. Burrowing owls hide in underground homes. Rattlesnakes slither through the grasses.

Between the grasslands and the lofty mountain peaks are the foothills. The foothills are filled with forests of scrub oaks, juniper, sagebrush, and pines. Raccoons and skunks feed on berries and nuts there.

Between 8,000 and 10,000 feet (2,400 m and 3,000 m) above sea level, quaking aspens, pines, and Douglas firs grow. Deer and elk graze in mountain meadows. Bears feast on berries, and hungry mountain lions stalk quick hares and deer.

The timberline is the place above which trees do not grow. In the southern

FROM WILLIAM CLARK'S JOURNAL
President Thomas Jefferson sent Meriwether Lewis and William Clark to explore the American West. In 1805, the Shoshone Indians told Lewis and Clark about the difficulties of traveling along the Columbia River through the Rockies. The Native Americans said that the mountains were so close to the river that it was hard to get through. Clark wrote that they also told him, "No deer, elk, or any game was to be found in that country. . . . There was no timber on the river sufficiently large to make small canoes."

Each spring, bighorn rams crash head-to-head for the right to mate with the ewes.
The sound echoes through Rocky Mountain canyons.

Rockies, that line is at about 11,500 feet (3,500 m). Farther north, in

the Canadian Rockies, the climate is colder, so the timberline is lower.

Above the timberline lies **tundra.** This is a cold ecosystem, but

it is not barren. Marmots, ptarmigan, and bighorn sheep thrive on the

alpine tundra. Wildflowers burst with color each spring, and moss and

lichen survive even under deep winter snows.

CHAPTER THREE

ABOUT THE ROCKIES

The Rocky Mountains run in a gentle curve from south to north. But there is nothing gentle about the Rockies. They block the West Coast from the rest of North America.

This mountain barrier stretches nearly 3,000 miles (4,800 km). The Rockies cover all or part of New Mexico, Colorado, Utah, Idaho, Wyoming, and Montana. In Canada, the mountains run through Alberta and end in British Columbia.

Pine forest covers the lower slopes of the southern Rockies.

Clusters of separate mountain ranges form the Rocky Mountain system. The Southern Rockies rise in New Mexico and end in Wyoming. The Middle Rockies include the Teton Mountains in Wyoming and in parts of Utah and Colorado, and they end at the Yellowstone River in Montana. The Northern Rockies include the mountains from Idaho to the Canadian border. In Canada, the Canadian Rockies stretch along the border between British Columbia and Alberta.

The Rockies' highest peaks rise more than 14,000 feet (4,300 m) above sea level. All of the 54 "fourteeners" lie in Colorado. The Rockies' tallest peak is Mount Elbert. Other major peaks include Mount Massive, Mount Harvard, and La Plata Peak. The tallest peak in the Canadian Rockies is Mount Robson, at 12,972 feet (3,954 m).

Glaciers cap many peaks in the Rocky Mountains. They fill river valleys and spread out over the foothills. Sometimes, glaciers join

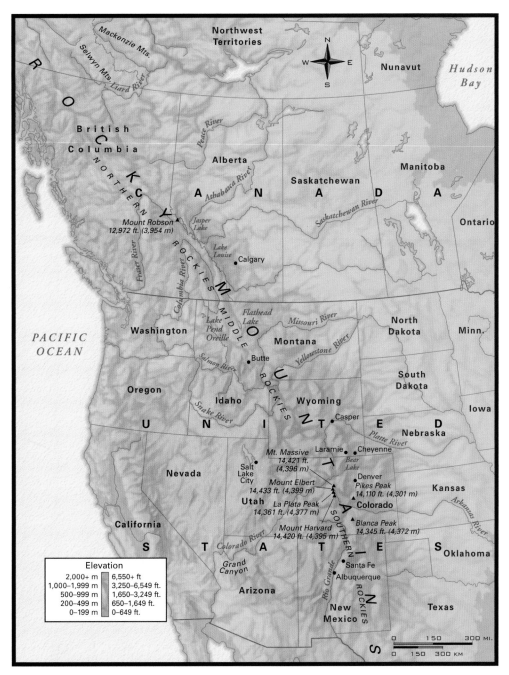

A map of the Rockies

to form massive ice fields, such as the Columbia Ice Field, on the

border between Alberta and British Columbia.

Spring wildflowers dance in the gentle breeze beside this peaceful mountain lake.

Some of North America's largest rivers begin in the Rocky Mountains. The Missouri, the Platte, and the Arkansas rivers begin in the Rockies and empty into the Mississippi River. The Rio Grande, which runs between the United States and Mexico, also begins in the Rockies. Rivers that flow west from the Rockies include the Columbia, the Salmon, and the Snake. In Canada, the Fraser empties into the Pacific.

Scenic lakes dot the Rockies from Colorado north into Canada toward Alaska. Many lakes in the Brooks, Selwyn, and Mackenzie ranges remain frozen all year. Farther south in Canada, Jasper Lake and Lake Louise have become major vacation spots. Bear Lake and Flathead Lake are important Rocky Mountain lakes in the United States.

CHAPTER FOUR

PLANTS AND ANIMALS
OF THE ROCKIES

The Rocky Mountains support a number of different ecosystems. The ecosystems vary according to climate and height above sea level. Still, most mammals and birds found in the Yukon are also found in New Mexico.

Large plant-eating animals thrive in Rocky Mountain meadows in

American bison nearly became extinct about 100 years ago.
Today, they thrive in preserves and on private ranches.

the summer. As winter comes, they move down the mountainside for food and shelter. Elk, moose, mule deer, and bison are among the largest plant eaters in the Rockies. Rocky Mountain bighorn sheep prefer to live on the tundra cliffs. They feed on moss, lichen, and grasses.

These large plant eaters attract large **predators.** In the Rockies, major predators include mountain lions and wolves. Wolves must hunt in a group to bring down an elk or bison. Smaller predators, such as coyotes, lynx, bobcats, and foxes, prey on hares, marmots, and pikas. They hunt by themselves and cannot handle large prey.

Both American black bears and grizzly bears make their home in the Rockies. They glut themselves on berries in late summer and fall. They fish for salmon in northern rivers. Bears will eat everything. The Rockies provide a full range of fruit, insects, nuts, fish, and other food for hungry bears.

Small mammals live most everywhere in the Rockies. Beavers build dams along mountain streams. Their ponds attract muskrats, otters, and weasels. Tiny shrews, meadow voles, and ground squirrels

This pair of gray wolves forms the basis of a pack in Yellowstone National Park. The male, lying down, is called the Alpha and is the pack leader.

scurry through lush summer meadows. Chipmunks, gophers, and hares scoot among the pines and aspens. High in the tundra, pocket gophers, pikas, and marmots build safe burrows to survive the long winter.

Songbirds play their part in the mountain food cycle. They feed on nuts,

WOLVES RETURN TO YELLOWSTONE

Between 1918 and 1935, the U.S. government paid hunters to kill all the wolves and coyotes in Yellowstone National Park. The government thought that the wolves killed too many bison, elk, and deer. In fact, gray wolves keep herds of these animals healthy. They kill mostly weak, sick, or old animals.

In 1995, the government returned gray wolves to Yellowstone. The 14 wolves that were released formed three packs. The program was a success. The wolves established territories and hunted elk and bison. Today, park rangers estimate 115 gray wolves live in Yellowstone.

Ground birds such as the ptarmigan have coloring that blends in with their environment. Hungry predators can not easily see this bird against the snow.

SNAKE RIVER BIRDS OF PREY

The Snake River Birds of Prey National Conservation Area in Idaho supports several hundred pairs of nesting raptors. In this preserve, golden eagles, falcons, hawks, harriers, kestrels, burrowing owls, and dozens of other raptor species thrive. They build cliff-side or ground nests. The birds hunt ground squirrels, jackrabbits, and other high desert animals.

berries, and insects. In turn, raptors and small predators feed on them. Squawking jays, western bluebirds, and hermit thrushes bicker over ripening berries. A three-toed woodpecker rat-a-tat-tats against a piñon pine to find insects. In the tundra, white ptarmigan survive long, cold winters.

Plant life flourishes in the Rockies. In the southern regions, piñon and bristlecone pines stretch over the landscape. Quaking aspens, cottonwoods, and birch dominate the banks of Colorado streams. Farther north, lodgepole and ponderosa pines rise straight and tall. Wildflowers such as purple-blue lupines, columbines, bright yellow buttercups, and goldenrod sprinkle color over open meadows.

In the Brooks, Selwyn, and Mackenzie ranges, tundra plants hug close to the ground. Sedges, lichens, and mosses are common. Summer brings a quick burst of color from pink saxifrage, purple arctic lupines, and yellow cinquefoil.

Efforts to preserve nature in the Rockies are many. The United States and Canada have established national parks, preserves, and wildlife refuges. Jasper and Banff national parks are among Canada's most popular parks. In Alaska, the Arctic National Wildlife Refuge safeguards the nesting sites of millions of ducks, geese, and plovers. Elsewhere in the United States, Yellowstone, Glacier, Grand Teton, and Rocky Mountain national parks are among the most famous parks. Dozens of other national and state parks also dot the Rockies.

CHAPTER FIVE

PEOPLE OF THE ROCKIES

People first came to the Rocky Mountain regions about 12,000 B.C. Over time, humans moved slowly southward. The earliest traces of humans in the Colorado Rockies are from about 10,000 years ago. These early people were hunter-gatherers. They hunted large animals and collected roots, berries, and nuts. These people did not build settled villages. Instead, they moved as the animals they hunted moved.

People began settling in villages in the Rockies around A.D. 500. These people were farmers. They planted corn, beans, and squash. Tourists can visit ruins of some of these villages in Colorado and New Mexico.

Modern Native American groups descended from these early peoples. The Rockies became home to the Shoshone, the Ute, and the Nez Percé, among others. Native Americans in the Rockies lived close to the land. They farmed and hunted and showed great respect for nature.

The Spanish and French first arrived in the Rockies in the 1600s. They were few in number and had little impact on the Native Americans who lived there. Then, gold was discovered in California in 1848. After that, thousands of wagon trains poured across the Great Plains and through the Rocky Mountains. Forts and trading posts sprang up along the route. Denver, Colorado, and Laramie and Cheyenne,

Ancient ruins show how early cultures lived in adobe or stone homes.

Wyoming, became centers for miners and ranchers. Santa Fe and Albuquerque, New Mexico, were outposts on the southern route to California. Suddenly, white families had come to the Rockies to stay.

MOUNTAIN MEN

The rugged mountain men were among the first white people to venture into the Rockies. Beginning in the 1820s, they traveled into the mountains to trap animals for their furs. Entirely alone, they faced the dangers of the Rockies. They confronted freezing weather and wild animals. Once a year, they would gather together at a big meeting called a rendezvous. There they would trade furs and swap stories. The mountain men helped open up the Rockies for the settlers who came later. And with their wild lives, they became legends.

The U.S. government made treaties with Native Americans. They set aside land for **reservations.** Often, the soil on the reservations was not good for growing crops, and there were few animals for hunting. And the borders of the reservations lasted only until white settlers wanted the Native American land. When settlers began demanding reservation land, the U.S. government took it back from the Native Americans. After many broken promises, some Native Americans went to war. The wars lasted several years, but the U.S. Army finally defeated the Indians.

Today, many Native American groups have reservations in the Rocky Mountains and its foothills. Some of these are the Ute Mountain Reservation in Colorado, the Flathead and Blackfeet reservations in Montana, and the Wind River Reservation in Wyoming.

Few major cities developed in the Rocky Mountains. The land is too rugged, and some places are too remote for large cities to thrive. Calgary, Alberta, is the largest Canadian city in the Rocky Mountains. Calgary is known for its annual "stampede." The 10-day

It looks like the bronco is going to beat the cowboy in this rodeo contest.

stampede is in fact a rodeo. It attracts calf ropers, chuck wagons, bull riders, and thousands of visitors. Tourists also go to Calgary because of the nearby skiing, white-water rafting, and Banff National Park.

Mile-high Denver is the largest American city in the Rockies. It is a center for manufacturing, cattle, mining, and agriculture. Denver provides easy access to Rocky Mountain ski resorts. It is also home to professional football, basketball, baseball, and hockey teams.

Mining is a major industry in the Rocky Mountains. Lead, tin,

Whitewater rafting is nature's roller coaster over these swift rapids.

tungsten, uranium, copper, silver, gold, and petroleum are all mined in

the Rockies. In addition, timber companies cut and mill lumber.

Tourism is an expanding business in the Rockies. Skiing, white-water

rafting, hiking, fishing, and camping attract millions of visitors to the

Rocky Mountains each year.

CHAPTER SIX

CULTURE OF THE ROCKIES

In the Rocky Mountains, Native American customs mix with the rowdy Wild West. Cities have their museums, concert halls, movie theaters, and universities. But the real Rocky Mountains cannot be found in city life.

The Rockies provide breathtaking scenery. Still lakes reflect the snowcapped peaks of the Grand Tetons and Glacier National Park.

Still water reflects the beauty of a Rocky Mountain morning.

Living in remote mining cabins protected prospectors from thieves.

Lake Louise and Lake Jasper come alive with the summer's flurry of ducks, geese, and swans.

Hikers in Mesa Verde National Park or Yellowstone may come upon delicate wildflowers, sheer rock cliffs, or a doe and her fawn grazing in a meadow. Visitors to the Yukon delight as a trail of caribou follow ancient paths through the tundra.

People in the Rockies remember the past. In Old West ghost towns, visitors recall a time when miners and their mules poured over the mountains. In other towns, rodeos draw cowboys for roping and riding. A Native American powwow presents Ute or Shoshone or Nez Percé customs and culture. Mountain men gatherings re-create the lives of these legendary fur trappers.

Many artists have tried to portray the beauty and mood of the

Rockies. Photographers capture grizzlies fishing in a stream. Painters catch the red-gold sun setting behind Utah's high desert. Turquoise and silver jewelry reflect clear New Mexico skies.

Music is as much a part of the Rockies as grizzly bears and ponderosa pines. Each year, the Rocky Mountain Ragtime Festival in Boulder, Colorado, features tinkling pianos and tooting trumpets. The Canadian Rocky Mountain Festival presents jazz, choirs, and symphony orchestras—all at the same event. For those who prefer playing to listening, bring nimble fingers to the Rocky Mountain Fiddle Camp.

Native American drums pound out a rhythm for dancers in traditional costume. This music and dance recall a time when Native American life was at one with nature. Travel into the wilderness of the Rocky Mountains today, and that spirit remains.

ALBERT BIERSTADT

The painter and photographer Albert Bierstadt came to the United States from Germany at the age of two and grew up in New Bedford, Massachusetts. In 1859, Bierstadt toured Colorado and Wyoming. After that, he returned to his home in New York City and painted landscapes of the Rocky Mountains. Though he had spent only a few weeks in the Rockies, he became famous as a "western" artist.

Glossary

ecosystems (EE-koh-siss-tuhms) An ecosystem is the community of plants, animals, water, and soil located in one area, which work together as a unit.

erosion (i-ROH-zhuhn) Erosion is the process of wearing away. Water erosion creates canyons as the water wears away the rock and soil.

glaciers (GLAY-shurz) Glaciers are huge sheets of moving ice.

igneous (IG-nee-uhss) Igneous describes a type of rock that is created when the material from a volcano cools underground.

magma (MAG-muh) Magma is the molten rock inside Earth. When magma cools, it becomes igneous rock.

metamorphic (met-uh-MOR-fik) Metamorphic describes a rock that has changed from one form to another over a period of time.

predators (PRED-uh-turz) Predators are animals that hunt and eat other animals.

raptors (RAP-turz) Raptors are birds that live by hunting and eating meat. Eagles, falcons, and vultures are raptors.

reservations (rez-ur-VAY-shuhnz) Reservations are pieces of land set aside forNative Americans to live and work.

sedimentary (sed-uh-MEN-tuh-ree) Sedimentary rock is formed from the remains of eroded mountains, including sand, clay, rock, salts, and animal remains. Limestone is a type of sedimentary rock.

species (SPEE-sheez) A species is a kind of plant or animal.

tundra (TUHN-druh) Tundra is a treeless region in the far north or on the upper portion of a mountain.

A Rockies Almanac

Extent

    Length: About 3,000 miles (4,800 km)

    Width: About 350 miles (560 km)

Continent: North America

Countries: Canada and United States

Major ranges: Brooks, Canadian Rockies, Mackenzie, Middle Rockies, Northern Rockies, Selwyn, and Southern Rockies

Major rivers: Arkansas, Athabasca, Colorado Columbia, Fraser, Liard, Missouri, Peace, Platte, Rio Grande, Salmon, Saskatchewan, Snake, Yellowstone, and Yukon

Major lakes: Bear, Flathead, Jasper, Louise, and Pend Oreille

Major cities: Butte (Montana); Calgary (Alberta); Cheyenne (Wyoming); Denver (Colorado); Salt Lake City (Utah)

Major languages: English

Highest peaks:

Mount Elbert	14,433 feet (4,399 m)
Mount Massive	14,421 feet (4,396 m)
Mount Harvard	14,420 feet (4,395 m)
La Plata Peak	14,361 feet (4,377 m)
Blanca Peak	14,345 feet (4,372 m)

Parks and preserves: Banff, Jasper (Canada); Glacier, Grand Teton, Rocky Mountain, Yellowstone (United States)

Natural resources: Coal, copper, gold, hydroelectric power, iron ore, lead, petroleum, silver, timber, tungsten, uranium, and zinc

Native birds: Eagles, falcons, hawks, harriers, hermit thrushes, jays, kestrels, owls, ptarmigans, three-toed woodpeckers, and western bluebirds

Native fish: Salmon

Native mammals: Beavers, bighorn sheep, bison, black bears, bobcats, caribou, chipmunks, coyote, deer, elk, foxes, gray wolves, grizzly bears, ground squirrels, hares, lynx, marmots, moose, mountain lions, muskrats, otters, pikas, pocket gophers, prairie dogs, shrews, voles, and weasels

Native reptiles: Rattlesnakes

Native plants: Aspens, birches, bristlecone pines, buttercups, cinquefoils, columbines, cottonwoods, Douglas firs, goldenrods, junipers, lodgepole pines, lichens, lupines, mosses, pinon pines, ponderosa pines, sagebrushes, saxifrages, sedges, and scrub oaks

The Rockies in the News

2 billion years ago	The Rocky Mountain region is uplifted for the first time.
500 million years ago	The Rocky Mountain region is uplifted a second time.
70 million years ago	A third uplift occurs and produces today's Rocky Mountains.
12,000 B.C.	Humans enter the Rockies.
A.D. 500	Humans first settle villages in the Rocky Mountains.
1804–1806	Lewis and Clark explore from the Missouri River to the Pacific Ocean.
1806	Zebulon Pike sights what is now Pikes Peak.
1848	The gold rush begins after gold is discovered in California; wagon trains begin passing through the Rockies.
1859	Albert Bierstadt visits Wyoming and Colorado; he becomes a painter of western landscapes.
1869	The transcontinental railroad is completed; people can travel more easily through the Rocky Mountains.
1872	Yellowstone becomes the first national park in the United States.
1918–1935	Wolves and coyotes are eliminated from Yellowstone.
1964	The U.S. government passes the Wilderness Act, which establishes new wilderness preserves.
1995	Gray wolves are reintroduced to Yellowstone National Park.

How to Learn More about the Rockies

At The Library
Nonfiction

Bograd, Larry. *The Rocky Mountains.* Tarrytown, N.Y.: Benchmark Books, 2001.

Jameson, W. C. *Buried Treasures of the Rocky Mountain West: Legends of Lost Mines, Train Robbery Gold, Caves of Forgotten Riches, and Indians' Buried Silver.* Little Rock, Ark.: August House Publishing, 2003.

Leach, Michael. *Grizzly Bear: Habitats, Life Cycles, Food Chains, Threats.* Austin, Tex.: Raintree/Steck-Vaughn, 2001.

Patent, Dorothy Hinshaw. *The Bald Eagle Returns.* Boston: Houghton Mifflin, 2000.

Sabin, Louis. *Narcissa Whitman: Brave Pioneer.* Mahwah, N.J.: Troll Communications, 1997.

Fiction

Kathren, Ginger. *Cloud: Wild Stallion of the Rockies.* Irvine, Calif.: Bowtie Press, 2001.

Lawlor, Laurie. *Crossing the Colorado Rockies 1864.* New York: Aladdin Press, 1999.

On the Web

Visit our home page for lots of links about the Rockies:
http://www.childsworld.com/links.html

Note to Parents, Teachers, and Librarians: We routinely verify our Web links to make sure they're safe, active sites—so encourage your readers to check them out!

Places to Visit or Contact

National Bison Range
132 Bison Range Road
Moiese, MT 59824
406/644-2211

Rocky Mountain Arsenal National Wildlife Refuge
U.S. Fish and Wildlife Service
Building 111
Commerce City, CO 80022-1748
303/289-0232

Index

About the Author

Barbara A. Somervill is the author of many books for children. She loves learning and sees every writing project as a chance to learn new information or gain a new understanding. Somervill grew up in New York State, but she has also lived in Toronto, Canada; Canberra, Australia; California; and South Carolina. She currently lives with her husband in Simpsonville, South Carolina.